W9-ABN-526

the science of CATASTROPHE

ECOLOGICAL DISASTERS

STEVE PARKER & DAVID WEST

Crabtree Publishing Company

www.crabtreebooks.com

Crabtree Publishing Company

www.crabtreebooks.com

Created and produced by:
 David West Children's Books
Project development and concept:
 David West Children's Books
Authors: Steve Parker and David West
Editor: Adrianna Morganelli
Proofreader: Crystal Sikkens
Designer: David West
Illustrator: David West
Project coordinator: Kathy Middleton
Production and print coordinator: Katherine Berti
Prepress technician: Katherine Berti

Library and Archives Canada Cataloguing in Publication

Parker, Steve, 1952-
 Ecological disasters / Steve Parker and David West.

(The science of catastrophe)
Includes index.
Issued also in electronic formats.
ISBN 978-0-7787-7573-7 (bound).--ISBN 978-0-7787-7578-2 (pbk.)

 1. Environmental disasters--Juvenile literature. I. West, David, 1956-
II. Title. III. Series: Science of catastrophe

GE140.5.P37 2011   j363.7   C2011-905008-0

Library of Congress Cataloging-in-Publication Data

Parker, Steve, 1952-
 Ecological disasters / Steve Parker & David West.
  p. cm. -- (The science of catastrophe.)
 Includes index.
 ISBN 978-0-7787-7573-7 (reinforced library binding : alk. paper) --
ISBN 978-0-7787-7578-2 (pbk. : alk. paper) -- ISBN 978-1-4271-8856-4
(electronic pdf) -- ISBN 978-1-4271-9759-7 (electronic html.)
 1. Pollution--Environmental aspects--Juvenile literature. 2. Nature--Effect of
human beings on--Juvenile literature. 3. Environmental disasters--Juvenile
literature. I. West, David. II. Title. III. Series.

 QH545.A1P36 2011
 363.7--dc23

                    2011027738

Crabtree Publishing Company

www.crabtreebooks.com   1-800-387-7650

Printed in the U.S.A./112011/JA20111018

Published in Canada
Crabtree Publishing
616 Welland Ave.
St. Catharines, Ontario
L2M 5V6

Published in the United States
Crabtree Publishing
PMB 59051
350 Fifth Avenue, 59th Floor
New York, New York 10118

Published in the United Kingdom
Crabtree Publishing
Maritime House
Basin Road North, Hove
BN41 1WR

Published in Australia
Crabtree Publishing
3 Charles Street
Coburg North
VIC 3058

Contents

Desertification

From 1930, North American prairie farms suffered a series of severe droughts. The soil had been worked too hard by crops and livestock. Within a few years it had gone— some blown as far as the ocean.

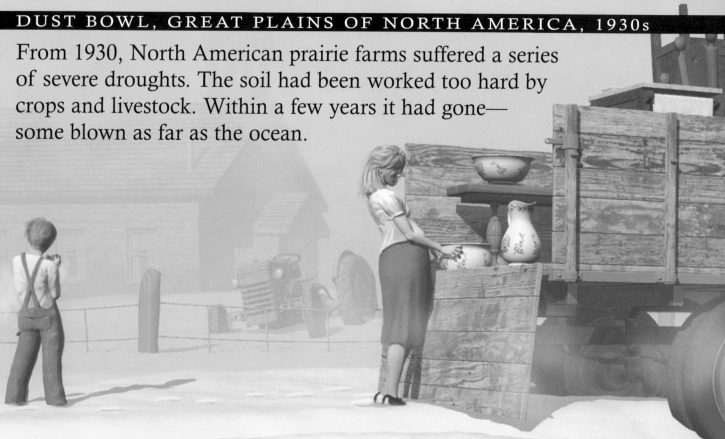

As pioneers pushed west across North America through the 1800s, they found wide-open prairie grasslands that seemed too dry for their traditional European farming methods. But by the 1900s, with new railroads and roads, more settlers arrived, keen for land of their own. The weather at this time was unusually wet, with plentiful rains. Plowed fields, cattle, and sheep spread fast. The soil seemed full of goodness, and old ideas such as **crop rotation** to save its nutrients faded away.

In 1930 the drought years began. Without natural grasses to hold moisture for months and years, the land began to dry. Deep plowing, crops, and grazing animals had taken the nutrients.

As regular winds swept past, they picked up the small soil particles like dust and desert sand, and carried them along. The whole region became a vast "bowl" of dust.

During the worst dust storms, the daytime sky was dark. People could see just a few feet. Dust blew into, and settled on, everything. By 1935 it was being carried as far as the East Coast, into the Atlantic Ocean. Hungry, broke farmers packed up the few possessions they had, and left for food and work elsewhere. By 1940 more than 2.5 million homeless Americans deserted the Great Plains area. Sadly, even today, turning good land into dusty desert still happens, especially in Africa.

An Oklahoma farming family leave the drought-stricken "Dust Bowl" and head west to California. (Artist's depiction)

THE SCIENCE OF DESERTIFICATION

Each region or **habitat** has its own natural vegetation and **ecology**, with plants well adapted to the conditions. Prairie grasses are suited to windy, dry conditions. The grass stems and dense roots take up and hold scarce moisture, and keep the soil in position despite the strong winds that whip across the open land. Poor farming methods plow the natural long-lived grasses, destroy their roots, and grow short-lived crops which are soon harvested, leaving the surface bare. Cattle and other animals graze the grasses to death. The soil becomes dry, loose, dusty, and easily carried away by strong winds.

1. On natural prairies, the well-adapted native grasses and their thick root networks keep soil moist and stable. Wind cannot blow it away.

2. Intensive farming plows the soil every year and reduces its nutrients. Too many grazing livestock also remove the natural grass cover.

3. Without the natural grasses and their roots, water dries quickly and the soil becomes dust. Sweeping winds soon blow away the loose particles.

*Fireboats tackle the blaze
on* Deepwater Horizon.
(Artist's depiction)

Oil Spill

On April 20, 2010, about 40 miles (65 kilometers) from the Louisiana coast, U.S.A., *Deepwater Horizon* was drilling a borehole to look for oil. A sudden fire killed 11 workers, injured 16, and triggered one of the worst oil spills ever.

Just before 10 a.m., a "blowout" surge of natural gas up the drill pipe caused a fire and explosion on the rig deck. The 115 survivors (including the injured) were quickly rescued, but firefighters could not contain the blaze, and the rig sank on April 22. The well head far below should have shut automatically. But a sequence of cost-cutting, time-saving problems meant, among other problems, the blowout preventer was faulty. Two days later, coastguards reported leaking oil. It coated the seabed and formed giant slicks that

drifted toward the shore. Several attempts to seal the leak failed as it gushed 2.6 million gallons (9.8 million liters) daily. On July 15 the well head was sealed by a temporary cap, with final closure by September 19. Despite massive clean-up efforts, thick, dark oil devastated sea and shore wildlife ecology, coastal fisheries, shrimping grounds, and vacation centers—and will continue to do so for many years.

THE SCIENCE OF OIL SPILLS

Deepwater Horizon was a 400-foot (122-meter) long, semi-submersible rig exploring oil reserves in an area known as the Mocando Prospect. Due to a series of faults, a slug of high-pressure natural gas rose up the drill pipe and spread across the deck. Containing methane and other **flammable** gases, it ignited in an explosion and fierce fire. Two days later the whole rig sank, allowing the well head on the seabed to release thick, sticky oil.

1. pressure at seabed and within rock layers forces oil up riser pipe

2. gas bubble in oil is released on deck, spark causes explosion

3. rig sinks, oil gushes through failed well head valve on seabed

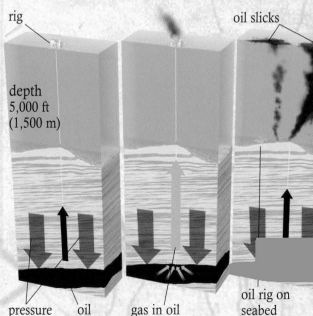

rig

oil slicks

depth 5,000 ft (1,500 m)

pressure   oil   gas in oil   oil rig on seabed

Loggers cut-and-clear yet another section of the not-so-vast Amazon Rain Forest. (Artist's depiction)

THE SCIENCE OF FOREST LOSS

Tropical forests are a vital part of the world's **ecosystem**. Their trees both take in carbon dioxide (CO_2), lessening the amounts of this **greenhouse gas** in the atmosphere, and make the oxygen (O_2) that all living things need. Trees also soak up sudden rainstorms preventing floods, then release the water slowly as vapor. Their roots also stabilize the soil. Deforestation destroys all these benefits.

Deforestation

People have long relied on forests for foods, building materials, medicines, and shelter. But in today's overcrowded, industrialized world, forests disappear at a terrifying rate—especially magnificent rainforest "hotspots."

Tropical rain forests are known as **biodiversity hotspots**. They are home to a wider range or diversity of plants and animals than anywhere else on Earth, with more than half of them known species. About 150 years ago, these forests covered about one-seventh of the world's land. Since then, more than half are gone. Today's loss rate each year is an area the size of New York State. If this deforestation continues, most of the rest could disappear within 50 years.

The chief human-made causes of tropical deforestation are cutting trees for valuable hardwood timber; drilling quarries and mines for oil, coal, and minerals; clearing land for crops and ranching, fires, and clearance for roads, towns, factories, and homes. Often these are combined. Loggers move in for timber, the remaining debris is set on fire, then cattle or crops such as palm-oil trees are brought in. Often, these activities are illegal, but officials ignore the harm because they get payments and favors from loggers, ranchers, farmers, and mine bosses. It is not just forest loss, with its tens of thousands of amazing creatures and plants, that is so tragic. There are wider effects on the region's ecology, with increased erosion, floods, altered local weather, and long-term climate change.

trees take in Sun's light and heat

water vapor evaporates slowly from trees

plants take in CO_2 and produce O_2

rainwater soaks in and is held

some of Sun's heat reflects into atmosphere

less water evaporates

less CO_2 removed from atmosphere

animals and plants disappear

rainwater drains away faster

huge variety of animals and plants

FORESTED   tree roots hold soil in place

DEFORESTED

farming destroys thin soil

loose soil washes away

Overfishing

"There's plenty more fish in the sea." But not any longer. Stocks, or numbers, of many important food fish have fallen hugely. It is no longer worth fishing boats searching for them, and some stocks may never recover.

Across the world's oceans, it is harder to catch fish. In Europe's North Sea, stocks of cod, herring, mackerel, plaice, and sole have been falling for 50 years. In the southwest Pacific Ocean, Peru's anchovy fisheries fell away in the 1970s. Over the Grand Banks off northwest North America, cod stocks collapsed in the 1990s. In the 2000s, the East China Sea's sharks, skates, and sturgeons were harder to find. There are similar tales around the globe, with many causes. Demand increases because more people turn to fish as a healthy food, and uses for leftover fishmeal increase, from pet foods to fertilizers.

Fishing boats get bigger and faster, with equipment such as **sonar** and **GPS** to find their prey. Huge pocket-like trawl nets drag across the ocean floor, scraping up almost everything and leaving dead zones in their wake. Giant curtain-like drift nets, called longlines, hang in the ocean, trapping all forms of marine life. Longlines are miles in length, with thousands of hooks.

Yet another fishing fleet heads into the Atlantic to kill hundreds more northern bluefin tuna. (Artist's depiction)

All these methods cause a terrible **bycatch** of unwanted animals such as seabirds, turtles, dolphins, porpoises, whales, seals, sharks, and other predatory fish who target the same food source. And the more fish caught, the more these big hunters starve.

In the Atlantic, the northern bluefin tuna is being fished to death. Since the 1970s, its numbers have plummeted by nine-tenths. Besides Japanese sashimi dishes and canned tuna, an extra threat is capturing the young to grow in fish farms. This leaves too few wild tuna to breed and keep up their numbers.

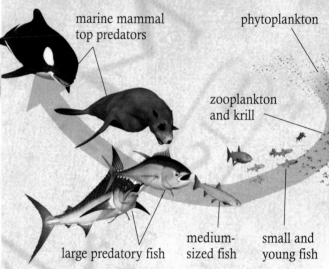

THE SCIENCE OF OCEANIC FOOD CHAINS

marine mammal top predators

phytoplankton

zooplankton and krill

large predatory fish

medium-sized fish

small and young fish

Like all creatures in nature, fish are part of complicated **food chains** on which life depends. These start with plants capturing the Sun's light energy. In the open sea the plants are tiny phytoplankton ("plant drifters"). These are consumed by tiny animals such as zooplankton and small shrimp-like krill. In turn these are eaten by larger fish and other animals, such as jellyfish and shellfish, and so on, up to the largest hunters like tuna, swordfish, sharks, and killer whales. If too many medium-sized fish disappear, food chains fall apart and the whole ecosystem suffers.

Famine

In a famine, some people do not die simply from lack of food. They perish from infections and other diseases brought on by poor nourishment. The worst famine of the past century occurred in China. It was due not only to droughts, floods, crop failures, and ecological disasters, but also to politics.

During the 1950s–60s, China went through vast changes, following the political idea called communism. Private possessions and making profits were frowned on. People shared everything, followed the government's orders, and worked for the good of everyone, in groups called collectives. Industry was favored, with workers ordered to move from farms to factories.

This seriously affected food production. Also many individuals could see no personal gain for their efforts, so they worked less hard. A new farming idea was to put crop plants closer together, but this simply made the plants weak, causing them to die. Then came three years of natural disasters. In 1958, floods hit much of the south. The next year, floods devastated huge areas around the Huang He (Yellow River) in China's northeast. In 1960, more than half the nation was affected by terrible droughts.

These disasters were made worse by government officials who followed orders so strictly that people in towns starved outside locked warehouses containing food.

To fight the famine, experts invented the Four Pests Campaign to kill off mosquitoes, flies, sparrows, and rats. But killing sparrows upset **food webs** and disturbed the ecology and balance of nature. It allowed pest insects to multiply and damage crops even more. In 1960–61 plagues of locusts made the disasters even worse. No one knows how many people suffered, starved, and finally died. It was at least 20 million, and maybe over 30 million.

A farming family try in vain to chase away bird pests in the Great Sparrow Campaign—not realizing this worsens their plight. (Artist's depiction)

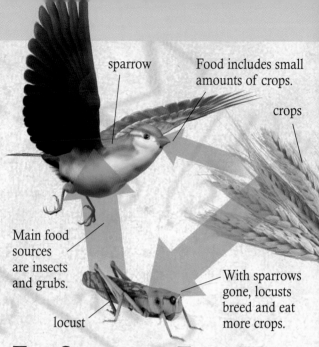

sparrow

Food includes small amounts of crops.

crops

Main food sources are insects and grubs.

With sparrows gone, locusts breed and eat more crops.

locust

THE SCIENCE OF FOOD WEBS

Very few animals eat just one kind of food. Most eat several kinds, especially through different seasons of the year. This joins food chains into food webs. In China's Great Sparrow Campaign of 1958–60, people were urged to shoot, trap, poison, and destroy sparrows, their nests, and young. But sparrows eat more insects, including crop pests, than crops. Removing them changed the food web so much that crop pests such as locusts thrived.

Global Warming

Earth has long had a natural greenhouse effect. Without it, average world temperatures would be below freezing. The problem is that modern energy use is making "greenhouse Earth" hotter, with dire prospects.

Earth's natural greenhouse effect is due to the heat-keeping effect of gases in the air of its atmosphere. Without it, average world temperatures would be way below freezing, at about 0 degrees Fahrenheit (minus 18 degrees Celsius). Since the end of the last Ice Age, around 12,000–10,000 years ago, the effect has kept long-term temperatures fairly steady. But this has changed in the past two centuries. Humans are putting extra amounts of the gas carbon dioxide, CO_2, into the atmosphere. It comes mainly from burning fuels, such as gas in automobiles, diesel in trucks, and kerosene in jets, to coal, oil, natural gas, and wood in homes, iron and steel plants, furnaces, factories, and power generators. The extra CO_2 is joined by other greenhouse gases like methane, from the guts of increasing numbers of cows, sheep, and pigs. The result is that world temperatures are creeping up, known as global warming.

Stranded on small melting icebergs, polar bears search for somewhere to rest and recover strength. (Artist's depiction)

Experts predict that in this century the temperature could rise 2.7–11 degrees Fahrenheit (1.5–6 degrees Celsius), depending on how much CO_2 and other gases we produce. The temperature rise is already melting icecaps and glaciers faster. The meltwater flows into the sea, causing its level to rise. Melting icebergs do not affect the sea level since they are already in the sea. But, like most substances, sea water itself gets bigger, or expands, as it becomes warmer. Its level could rise by 12 inches (30 centimeters) in 50 years, to cover low-lying coastal cities, shores, and farmland. As the oceans, land, and atmosphere heat up, this affects the climate. Likely changes include altered patterns of winds, clouds, and rainfall, and probably more extreme weather such as hurricanes, floods, and droughts.

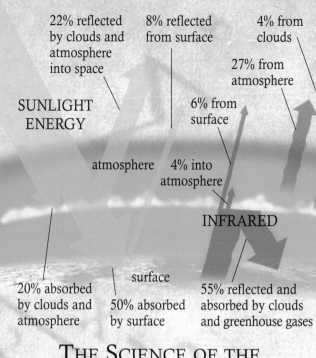

22% reflected by clouds and atmosphere into space

8% reflected from surface

4% from clouds

27% from atmosphere

SUNLIGHT ENERGY

6% from surface

atmosphere

4% into atmosphere

INFRARED

20% absorbed by clouds and atmosphere

surface

50% absorbed by surface

55% reflected and absorbed by clouds and greenhouse gases

THE SCIENCE OF THE GREENHOUSE EFFECT

Greenhouses (glasshouses) get warm because light waves come in easily, then their energy is absorbed and changed by objects and materials inside. This energy is given off, or re-radiated, as heat or infrared rays, which cannot escape back out through the glass. Earth's greenhouse effect works in a similar way, but with the air or atmosphere instead of glass panes. At the surface and in the atmosphere, some of the Sun's light is changed to heat or infrared. Increasing amounts of certain gases, especially carbon dioxide, are better at absorbing this heat and keeping it in the atmosphere, and so the temperature rises.

Plastic in the Oceans

Plastics are incredibly useful—and terribly harmful. Most kinds do not break up or decompose naturally. The bits hang around for hundreds or thousands of years. Millions are hanging around in the North Pacific.

The world's oceans are always on the move. There are many large flows called currents. Even greater are the five main gyres, which are huge circulating currents on a global scale. The North Pacific Gyre swirls clockwise around a vast area roughly centered on the Hawaiian Islands. Its waters gather all kinds of drifting trash and garbage from the Pacific coasts of East Asia and North America, from trees washed along rivers, to debris and pollution from beaches and harbors, and junk thrown overboard at sea. The gyre has a concentrating effect, bringing the mass of garbage into a vast floating patch up to 2,000 miles (3,200 kilometers) wide. Some of it, such as food leftovers, wood, and seaweed, decays naturally. Most of the plastics, such as bags, bottles, twine, and buoys, resist decay. Very gradually they crack into smaller pieces, the size of rice grains, then smaller still. These float in the topmost few feet (one–two meters) of water. Creatures such as fish, seabirds, turtles, dolphins, and whales eat objects they mistake for food, and suffer lingering deaths.

THE SCIENCE OF THE GREAT PACIFIC GYRE

Ocean currents are caused by a mix of winds, the Sun's heating effects, tides, coastline shapes, seabed depth and features, and the spinning motion of Earth, including the **Coriolis Effect**. The North Pacific Gyre combines four currents: Kuroshio, North Pacific, California, and North Equatorial. These slow down near the center of the gyre, allowing the garbage to collect.

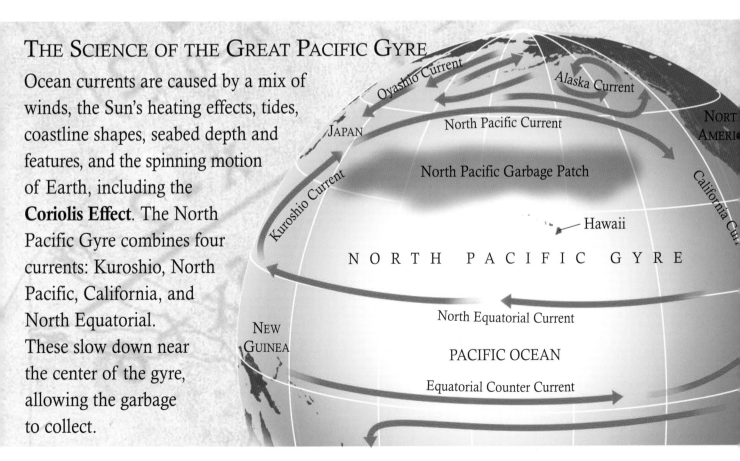

A sea turtle eats a plastic bag it mistakes for a jellyfish. (Artist's depiction)

Algal Bloom

Also known as "**toxic** tides" and "red tides," algal blooms are overgrowths of small, simple water plants called algae, and similar living things. The harmful substances they make get into food chains and do deadly damage.

Most life in the sea depends ultimately on light-capturing phytoplankton, which consists of tiny, floating life-forms such as diatoms, protists, and blue-green algae (not true algae, but living things known as cyanobacteria). In nature, their numbers are limited by the amounts of nutrients, minerals, and salts in the waters around them. Problems arise when there are too many nutrients, minerals, and salts, coming from fertilizers, sewage, and other sources on land. Some phytoplankton multiply fast, making extra amounts of their own waste substances.

These can be harmful or toxic to other life, such as fish, shellfish, and sea mammals. They may also stain the water red or brown.

In spring 2004, 107 bottlenose dolphins and many fish died along the coasts of Florida, U.S.A., due to a Florida Red Tide. The dolphins had eaten fish called menhaden. These, in turn, were affected by phytoplankton which made high levels of brevetoxin, a nerve poison. The toxin had been increased or concentrated along the food chain, to affect the dolphins' brains and nerves.

THE SCIENCE OF HARMFUL ALGAL BLOOMS (HABs)

Substances such as nitrates and phosphates are heavily used as farm fertilizers. They are washed by rain through the soil into rivers, and flow into the sea, known as **agricultural runoff**. Another source of excess nutrients is raw or untreated sewage put straight into the sea. These substances encourage blooms or overgrowths of plankton. Two well-known toxins are brevetoxin, made by *Karenia*, a protist (single-celled life-form), and domoic acid, produced by *Pseudo-nitzschia*, a diatom (single-celled alga or simple plant).

river carries runoff from farmland with nitrates (from fertilizers) and phosphates (from sewage) into sea

nitrogen from atmosphere

sunlight

algal bloom

algal bloom blocks sunlight, seawater beneath lacks oxygen, shellfish and other life die

Beach-goers make a tragic discovery of more than 100 dead and dying dolphins on the Florida coast. (Artist's depiction)

Invasive Species

The lists of plants and animals taken from their natural homes, to multiply and create havoc in a new habitat, grow longer each year. Australia has suffered hugely from these invasive species—especially the familiar rabbit.

In most wild areas, most of the time, native plants and animals live in a natural balance. However, in a new and different habitat, the natural restrictions on numbers may be missing. A new or alien species can breed unchecked and become an invasive species, causing massive damage to the local ecology. Rabbits were taken to Australia with the first

European settlers in the 1780s, probably caged as food. They did not seem to cause many problems until a small group, sent over from England, was released on a farm in the south of the country, in 1859. The farmer, Thomas Austin, said, "The introduction of a few rabbits could do little harm and might provide a touch of home, in addition to a

spot of hunting." With plenty of food, soft soil for their warren homes, warm winters, and lack of their natural predators, the rabbits bred and spread all over Australia's south and east. They ruined vast areas of farmland and natural bush. They were shot, poisoned, and trapped, but with almost no effect. Their numbers reached over 600 million. In the 1950s, a rabbit disease called myxomatosis was deliberately introduced as a form of **biological control**. This helped to reduce their numbers, but some rabbits since have become resistant to the disease.

Rabbits devastate the natural ecology of the Australian outback. (Artist's depiction)

THE SCIENCE OF INVASIVE SPECIES

The natural checks on a species in its native habitat include limited food and water, various diseases, restricted living space and shelter, competition with species who have similar ecological needs, and predators. Rabbits escaped many of these checks when they arrived in Australia. Red foxes were also taken from Europe to Australia, partly for hunting, and also to control the rabbits. But the foxes have also spread and devastated the native wildlife by eating local species.

Rabbits eat plants, leaving less food for local species and leading to desertification.

Farm animals lose pasture land.

Warrens create loose, unstable soil.

Banks wash away more easily due to warren tunnels.

Local species move away or become extinct.

*Dead fish litter the Rhine
River, which has been dyed
red by the chemical spill
from a storage center owned
by the Sandoz company.
(Artist's depiction)*

Freshwater Pollution

CHEMICAL SPILL, GERMANY, 1986

Pollution of any form harms the environment. But when dangerous industrial chemicals are spilled into a lake or river, the water life cannot escape. This happened to the Rhine River in Europe, in 1986.

Lakesides and riverbanks are convenient for towns and cities. Many factories have grown up along rivers too, where the water is used for washing and cleaning, chemical processes, and transport. In olden days, any old wastes were dumped in the river, often with terrible effects on the ecology and wildlife. In modern times, better laws and more regulations have gradually improved to protect the local environment. But accidents happen…

On November 1, 1986, a fire broke out in a warehouse of the chemical company Sandoz, in Schweizerhalle, northeast Switzerland. The origin of the blaze is unknown. But the result of the fire and the fight against it was a deadly mix of 30 tons (27 metric tons) of concentrated chemicals entering the Rhine River. These included a variety of insecticides and other pest-killers, also mercury chemicals, and colored dyes that stained the water. Local people were advised to stay indoors. Soon dead fish floated to the surface. The chemicals flowed north in the river, through Germany. They were designed to kill flies, mites, and other crop pests. But they were so powerful that they harmed fish, shellfish, water snails, worms, and waterbirds, for at least 100 miles (160 kilometers). The river took several years to recover.

THE SCIENCE OF FRESHWATER POLLUTION

Pollution gets into streams, rivers, pools, and lakes from many sources. Once in a lake or slow-flowing river, it may hang around for weeks and months. Even if it affects only some forms of life, for example, water insects, this upsets the natural balance. Animals that feed on the insects go hungry, or they take in the chemicals in the bodies of their prey, and themselves start to suffer.

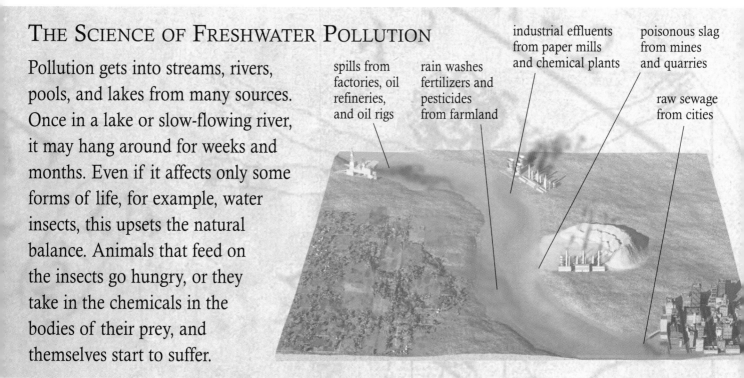

spills from factories, oil refineries, and oil rigs

rain washes fertilizers and pesticides from farmland

industrial effluents from paper mills and chemical plants

poisonous slag from mines and quarries

raw sewage from cities

Acid Rain

Winds, clouds, and rain do not stop at a country's border. Acid rain has been one of the most widespread and damaging forms of eco-pollution in the past century. Some controls have been introduced—but not enough.

Modern life relies on burning vast amounts of coal, oil, natural gas, and other **fossil fuels**, in all kinds of fires, furnaces, machines, and engines. As well as releasing greenhouse gases, other polluting substances include the chemicals sulfur dioxide and various nitrogen oxides. These are carried along by the wind, dissolve in clouds, and eventually fall as acid rain. As the rainwater enters the soil and waterways, it causes huge environmental problems. It damages trees and other plants by being taken up from soil through their roots, as well as falling directly on their leaves. It harms water life too, such as fish and shellfish.

Certain species are especially sensitive, such as spruce and maple trees, brook trout, and water snails. Not only wildlife suffers. In cities, acid rain eats away the stones, bricks, and metal in statues, roofs, walls, and other structures.

Because of wind patterns, this silent menace can wreak havoc far from the source of the pollution. For example, the factories, power plants, and crowded vehicles of Europe's industrial centers lead to acid rain over 1,000 miles (1,600 kilometers) to the east, in the remote forests of Poland, Belarus, and Ukraine. Trees lose their leaves, dead fish float in the water, and the damage lasts for years.

THE SCIENCE OF ACID RAIN

1. Burning fossil fuels releases pollutants, especially sulfur dioxide (SO_2) and nitrogen oxides.

2. Winds carry pollutants hundreds of miles.

3. Pollutants dissolve in cloud droplets, making them acidic.

4. Acid rain falls far away from the origin of pollution.

5. Soil, lakes, rivers, plants, and animals are all affected.

Acid rain poisons conifer forests and lakes in Poland, far from the pollution source. (Artist's depiction)

Sulfur dioxide and various nitrogen oxides, from fossil fuel burning, float into the air and blow with the wind. When they encounter tiny water droplets in clouds, the chemicals dissolve to turn the water into weak forms of sulfuric acid and nitric acid. The droplets eventually fall as acid rain, perhaps far away. This soaks in the soil, rivers, and lakes, and harms many living things.

Air Pollution

Like soil and water, air receives all kinds of polluting substances. Various smogs, hazes, and clouds dim the Sun and make breathing difficult. The biggest is the Asian Brown Cloud, which can hang around for three months.

One vehicle or home coal fire may not seem to add much to the atmosphere, but millions upon millions produce real problems. One of the most familiar is smog (smoke and fog) over big cities in sunny, calm weather. Sunlight acts on chemicals such as nitrogen oxides, produced especially by auto engines, also electricity generation, and factories fueled by coal and oil. The result is a floating haze of tiny particles and substances such as oxides, nitrates, aldehydes, and the gas ozone (see next page). In the human body these cause runny eyes and nose, breathing problems, and lower resistance to illness. Animals and plants are also affected.

From the 1990s, satellite photographs showed a vast brown "stain" across parts of South and Southeast Asia. This Asian or Atmospheric Brown Cloud is more than smog. It's due to a wide variety of air

Smog blankets Asian cities, blocking the Sun for weeks with stale, hazy air. (Artist's depiction)

pollution, from vehicle exhaust fumes to forest clearance by fires, even erupting volcanoes. The cloud forms early in the year, when winds are light, and there is little rain to remove the tiny drifting particles. It can last for more than three months, varying only slightly. It seems to get the most severe every three or four years, being smaller and less dense between. Local nations such as Pakistan, India, China, Thailand, and Indonesia aim to develop their industries, generate more power, and fill new roads with new vehicles. So the Brown Cloud may grow bigger and thicker in the future, and even affect climate, temperature, and rainfall.

THE SCIENCE OF AIR POLLUTION

Almost any kind of burning—from wood and coal fires, to vehicle engines, furnaces, factories, and power producers—sends fumes and particles into the air. In parts of Southeast Asia, huge forest fires begin accidentally, or they are part of tropical forest clearance for timber and farmland (as explained earlier). The same area has active volcanoes that can spew out gigantic amounts of ash and vapors as they erupt, adding natural air pollution to the human-made sources.

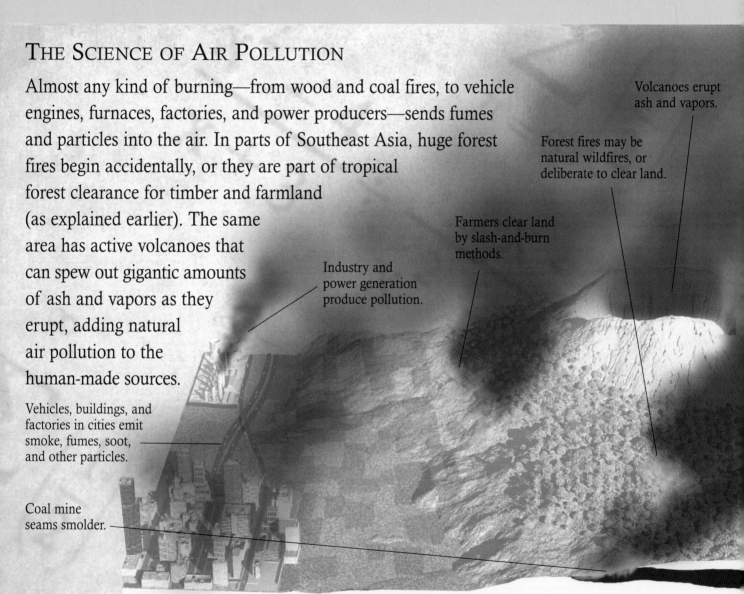

Volcanoes erupt ash and vapors.

Forest fires may be natural wildfires, or deliberate to clear land.

Farmers clear land by slash-and-burn methods.

Industry and power generation produce pollution.

Vehicles, buildings, and factories in cities emit smoke, fumes, soot, and other particles.

Coal mine seams smolder.

27

Space shuttles like Atlantis *have helped to measure thinned ozone around the world. The "holes" should repair by the year 2100. (Artist's depiction)*

Ozone Depletion

The gas ozone guards Earth's life against dangerous ultraviolet rays from the Sun. Less or depleted ozone, due to pollution of the atmosphere with human-made chemicals such as CFCs, is a serious hazard.

Ozone is a natural gas found high in the atmosphere. Each particle or molecule has three atoms of oxygen, O_3—one more than the usual form of oxygen gas, O_2. The ozone layer is like a shield, absorbing and removing the Sun's ultraviolet energy before it reaches the surface. This is vital, since too much ultraviolet greatly harms living things.

In 1985, a lack or depletion of ozone was discovered over Antarctica. It is not a true "ozone hole," but less or thinned ozone, mainly in winter and spring. More areas of thinning were found over the Arctic and other regions. The problem was largely due to chemicals called chlorofluorocarbons (CFCs), used especially in cooling and refrigerating equipment. As CFCs leaked or were released, they passed into the atmosphere and broke up in sunlight. This set free atoms of chlorine, each one able to break 100,000 molecules of ozone. The risk was more ultraviolet energy reaching the surface, causing damage to wildlife, farm crops and animals, and people. Known effects include skin cancer, eye damage, and failed crops, as well as killing plankton, which can hugely alter the ecology of the oceans. International laws are helping to bring the problem under control.

THE SCIENCE OF OZONE DEPLETION

Most ozone is found 12–25 miles (20–40 kilometers) high, mixed with other gases of the atmosphere, mainly nitrogen and oxygen. Ozone is created when the Sun's energy rays, especially ultraviolet rays, break apart the oxygen molecule allowing one oxygen atom to join with another oxygen molecule. The ozone absorbs, or takes in, most of the ultraviolet energy. As CFCs destroy ozone, they also remove its ultraviolet-shielding ability.

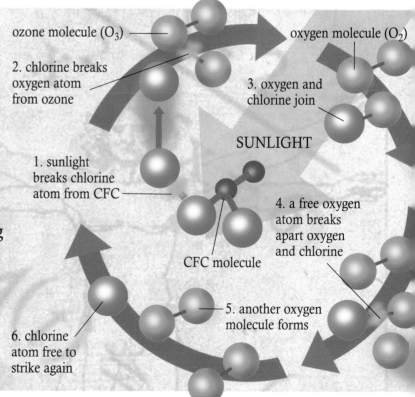

ozone molecule (O_3)

oxygen molecule (O_2)

2. chlorine breaks oxygen atom from ozone

3. oxygen and chlorine join

SUNLIGHT

1. sunlight breaks chlorine atom from CFC

4. a free oxygen atom breaks apart oxygen and chlorine

CFC molecule

5. another oxygen molecule forms

6. chlorine atom free to strike again

29

Disasters World Map

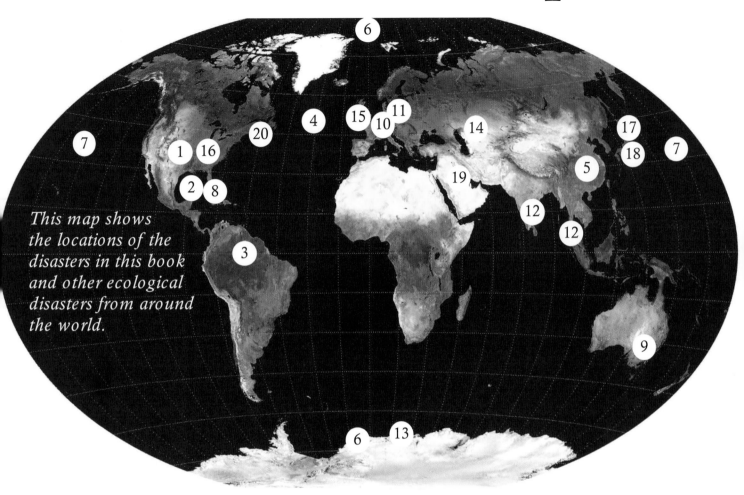

This map shows the locations of the disasters in this book and other ecological disasters from around the world.

1. Dust Bowl Desertification, Great Plains of North America, 1930s

2. *Deepwater Horizon* Oil Spill, Gulf of Mexico, 2010

3. Amazon Rainforest Deforestation, Brazil, 1970s Onward

4. Overfishing Northern Bluefin Tuna, North Atlantic, 1970s Onward

5. Great Chinese Famine, 1958–1962

6. Melting Ice Caps, Arctic and Antarctic, Ongoing

7. Great Pacific Garbage Patch of Plastic, North Pacific, 1988 Onward

8. Algal Bloom and Death of 107 Dolphins, Gulf of Mexico, 2004

9. Rabbits as an Invasive Species, Australia, From 19th Century Onward

10. Chemical Spill, Germany, 1986

11. Acid Rain and Dying Forests, Poland 1990s

12. Asian Brown Cloud, From 1990s

13. Ozone Depletion, Antarctica, 1980s Onward

14. Shrinking Aral Sea, Kazakhstan, 1960s Onward

15. Great Smog, United Kingdom, 1952

16. Tennessee Coal Sludge Spill, U.S.A., 2008

17. Fukushima I Nuclear Accident, Japan, 2011

18. Minamata Disease, Japan, 1950s–60s

19. Kuwaiti Oil Fires, 1991

20. Sydney Tar Ponds, Nova Scotia, Canada, 20th Century

Glossary

agricultural runoff Chemicals such as pesticides and fertilizers washed by rain through soil into rivers, lakes, and the sea

biodiversity hotspot An area with a very wide range or variety of living things

biological control Using one kind of living thing to control or limit the numbers of another, such as a predator introduced to eat a prey, which is an invasive species

bycatch Living things trapped or caught accidentally, such as in fishing nets, which are not the main target

Coriolis Effect The angled or twisting deflection given to moving objects due to the daily rotation of Earth

crop rotation Growing different crops each year, and sometimes none at all, to keep up the goodness of the soil and its nutrients

ecology The way animals, plants, and other living things exist and interact in their habitat or surroundings—"how nature works"

ecosystem A particular kind of living place or habitat, studied from the point of view of its ecology and how its animals, plants, soil, air, rocks, and other surroundings all interlink and interact

flammable Able to ignite or catch fire easily

food chain The series of feeding links whereby a plant is eaten by another animal, which is then consumed by another animal, and so on

food web How food chains link together when different animals eat a variety of foods

fossil fuels Fuels burned for energy, which come from the fossilized (preserved) remains of once-living things. The main forms are coal, oil (petroleum), and natural gas.

GPS Global Positioning System, a network of orbiting satellites that allow us to pinpoint our location anywhere on Earth

greenhouse gases Gases that increase the greenhouse effect and cause Earth's temperature to rise

habitat A particular kind of living place or surroundings, such as a pond, river, desert, conifer forest, or seashore

sonar Sound waves, which are detected and analyzed to show the distance and direction of the objects that made or reflected them

toxic Harmful or damaging to living things

Index